Questions and Answers

Space

A galaxy of fascinating facts and figures

Written by Diane Stephens

Introduction

How far away is space? Actually it is not that far away at all. The atmosphere of the Earth is only 900 km thick and above that space begins. If your family car could drive straight up you could be in space in a day.

After that short distance things start to get bigger, much, much bigger. Distances in space can get so big that they are often difficult to imagine. The Moon is 386,000 km away, which would take 268 days by car (without stopping for sleep or food), but the nearest star, Proxima Centauri, is forty million, million km away, which is just over 76 million years by car. To deal with these huge numbers scientists use light years, which is the distance light (the fastest possible speed) can travel in one year. By this measurement Proxima Centauri is only 4.2 light years away. Unfortunately space is so big that the furthest observable object is over ten billion light years away.

Everything inside the observable universe is ruled by gravity. Gravity keeps your feet on the ground. It keeps the Moon travelling round the Earth, and the Earth around the Sun. It keeps all the planets, right out to Pluto and beyond, in place. Amazingly, this force is very weak. Every time you pick up an object you are overcoming the gravitational pull of an entire planet! When things get big however, gravity becomes much more powerful. A black hole is gravity gone mad. Gravity in these collapsed stars is so powerful that even light cannot escape its pull, so they appear pitch black. These cosmic monsters devour everything that they come across. Luckily for us the nearest known black hole is over 1,600 light years away.

Eventually gravity will decide the fate of the entire universe. The universe started with the **Big Bang** (ten billion years ago) and it has been growing ever since. Scientists can measure this growth and are checking to see if the universe will continue to grow forever or if gravity will eventually pull it all back together again.

At the very edge of the universe is the cosmic background radiation. This is the leftover heat from the big bang that has not yet cooled down. Scientists can measure this radiation, and they use it to study the early days and even minutes of the universe. While this radiation is ten billion light years away you can see a little part of it by tuning your television (or radio) to an empty station. A small percentage of the hissing static on the screen is caused by the cosmic background radiation, a little part of the birth of the universe right there in your room.

Over thirty years of space. From the Apollo Moon landings to the latest deep space probe "New Horizons".

The image (left) shows Apollo 17 Astronaut, Eugene Cernan, saluting the US flag on the Moon during the last Apollo mission in 1973.

(Bottom left) The shuttle Atlantis blasting off from Cape Canaveral before the destruction of the Columbia suspended manned space missions.

(Below) An artist's impression of the New Horizons probe at the edges of the solar system amongst the comets of the remote Kuiper Belt.

The Earth

Crust Mantle Outer Mantle
Inner Core

What makes the Earth different from other planets?

The **planet** we live on is called Earth and it is the only planet we know of that has plants, animals and people. This is because the Earth has liquid water (it is the only planet with seas) and has **oxygen** in its atmosphere. Both of these are necessary for plants, animals and people to survive.

What is inside the Earth?

Scientists think the Earth was formed about 4.5 billion years ago. If we could cut the Earth open we would see different layers inside. On the outside is the crust covering a thick layer of very hot rock, the mantle. Beneath that is a layer of very hot, soft metal and in the middle of the Earth is the **core**, which is solid and made mostly of metal.

Moon

Why do we have calendars?

The Earth moves around the Sun in a huge circle called an **orbit.** It takes the Earth a year to orbit the Sun, moving at a very fast 106,000 km per hour. The Earth also spins around in a circle, turning once in 24 hours. If the Earth turned faster our days would be shorter. If the Earth turned more slowly, our days would be longer. Our calendar is based on these movements.

Sun

Why is Earth called the blue planet?

The atmosphere is the layer of air that surrounds the Earth. From space, the atmosphere looks like a thin layer of blue covering the planet. Although the atmosphere stretches about 900 km into space, it is relatively thin in comparison to the size of the Earth. If Earth was the size of an apple, the atmosphere would be about the thickness of the apple skin.

What is the only living organism on Earth that can be seen from space?

The Great Barrier Reef is a huge **coral reef** on the north-eastern coast of Australia, and is the only living organism that can be seen from outer space. It is larger than the United Kingdom and longer than the western coast of the United States.

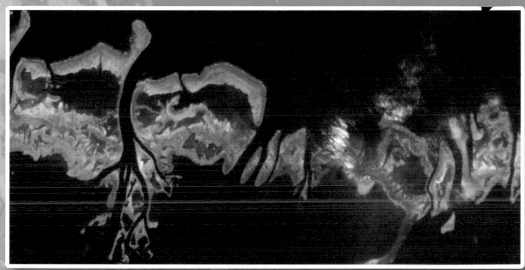

Part of the Great Barrier Reef, photographed from the Space Shuttle "Endeavour".

Why don't we float off the Earth?

Everything on Earth is pulled by an invisible force called gravity. It is what keeps you, animals, buildings and even the oceans from floating away into space. In space, far away from the Earth, Moons and stars, there is hardly any gravity which is why **astronauts** float.

Astronaut Ed White floats above the Earth.

Our Moon

Where did the Moon come from?

Nobody is certain, but it is thought that the Moon may have formed millions of years ago when the Earth was hit by a huge planet. Large pieces of rock broke off the Earth and went shooting into space. The rocks stayed in space, held by the Earth's gravity. Slowly the rocks joined together to form a very large Moon.

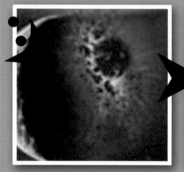

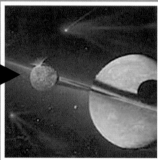

A body the size of Mars crashes into the Earth.

Trillions of tonnes of rock are thrown into space.

Gravity slowly forms the rocks into the Moon.

Why does the Moon change shape?

The Moon doesn't really change shape, it only looks as though it does from Earth. This is because as the Moon travels round the Earth (orbits), the Sun shines on a different part of the Moon each night. The changing shapes that we can see are known as the Moon's phases. It takes the Moon 27 days to orbit the Earth, and 27 days to spin around once.

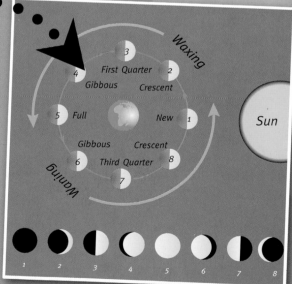

Waxing

First Quarter
Gibbous   Crescent
3   2
4
5   Full   New   1
Sun
Gibbous   Crescent
6   Third Quarter   8
Waning
7

1 2 3 4 5 6 7 8

What is the Moon like?

The Moon is a very different place to Earth. It has no air, water or life. There is no wind or rain either so that the footprints made by the first man on the Moon, Neil Armstrong, will be there for millions of years. There are huge craters on the surface of the Moon. Scientists think these were made by large rocks from space crashing into it. You can see these craters from Earth if you look at the Moon on a clear night.

What is a blue moon?

When we say "Once in a blue Moon", we mean not very often. Normally there is only one full Moon every month but occasionally there is a second "blue Moon". Because of the time it takes for the Moon to go from new to full, this only occurs once every two and a half years. A blue Moon is not really blue although sometimes the Moon can appear different colours after **volcanic eruptions** because of the dust in the air.

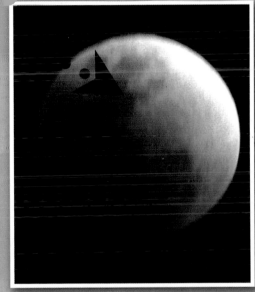

Volcanic dust in the air turns the Moon a deep red colour as seen from Mount Kitts Observatory.

Fun Fact!

Because there is no atmosphere on the Moon, sound waves cannot travel. So however loud you shouted, no one would be able to hear you!

How many people have been to the Moon?

Astronaut Buzz Aldrin follows Neil Armstrong onto the surface of the Moon.

In all, 12 people have visited the Moon. There were 6 missions to the Moon between 1969 and 1972. The first man to walk on the **Moon** was Neil Armstrong who famously said "One small step for man, one giant leap for mankind". On each visit the astronauts brought back Moon rock, a total of 380 kg and walked about 90 km of the Moon's surface.

What causes a lunar eclipse?

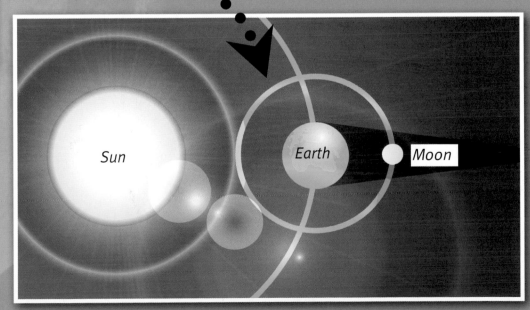

Sun
Earth
Moon

Sunlight casts a shadow on everything, including the Earth. A lunar eclipse happens when the Moon passes through the Earth's shadow. Very rarely when the Sun, Earth and Moon are all lined up, the Moon appears to completely disappear in the Earth's shadow.

Mars

What is Mars like?

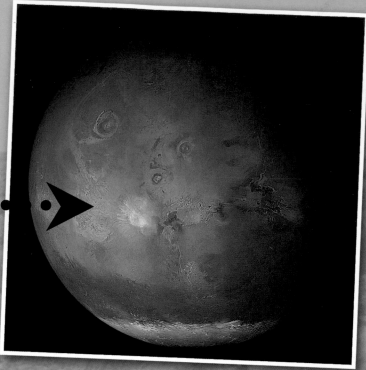

In many ways Mars is similar to the Earth. It has an atmosphere, weather and seasons. The atmosphere is very thin and made mostly of poisonous **carbon dioxide**. Gravity is much weaker so you would weigh much less on Mars. Because Mars is further from the Sun than the Earth it is much colder, only reaching around -28 degrees Celsius, which is about as cold as the North Pole.

Close up view of Mars showing the frozen southern ice cap. A Martian dust storm can be seen near the middle of the planet showing that Mars has both weather and winds.

Is there life on Mars?

In 1976 two Viking spacecraft landed on Mars to carry out **experiments**. They took samples of soil, which were tested, but no sign of life was found. Frozen water has now been found at the south pole of Mars, so it is possible that there is some form of life, however small. New spacecraft are due to land on Mars to see if there was life there long ago, or if any has survived under the surface as bacteria.

How many Moons does Mars have?

Mars has two Moons. Both are tiny and very dark so they were not discovered until 1877. The largest is called Phobos and is about 25 km across. The smaller Moon is called Deimos and is only 15 km across. In contrast our Moon is nearly 3,500 km wide. Both Moons have very low orbits and move very fast.

Phobos (top) is closest to its planet than any other Moon. Tiny Deimos (bottom) is the smallest Moons in the solar system.

Fun Fact!

It would take 66.5 years to travel from Earth to Mars travelling at 100 km per hour, but only 5 minutes travelling at the speed of light.

Why is Mars called the "Red Planet"?

The surface of Mars as seen by the cameras of the Mars rover Spirit, which landed on Mars in early 2004.

When you look at Mars in the night sky it appears a pale red colour. The surface of Mars is covered in rocks, boulders and sand. All these have a rusty red colour. Even the sky is red from dust blown around by the wind. All these rocks have a lot of iron in them. This iron has rusted over the years, giving the whole planet its distinctive colour.

Has anybody ever been to Mars?

No people have been to Mars yet but scientists have sent several **space probes**. The first probes to land, Viking 1 and 2 were large and could not move around. They carried TV cameras so that scientists could see what it looked like on the surface of Mars. Later, probes like Pathfinder carried small robots that moved over the surface.

Mars Pathfinder was the first mobile rover to land on Mars.

Above is an artist's impression of a possible early Mars settlement

Could people live on Mars?

Mars is probably the best place in the solar system for man to build bases, though life would be very difficult there. You would need to wear a space suit to go outside because of the cold and the poisonous air. There is plenty of frozen water on Mars so bases would have to be built near this at the poles. Over thousands of years people could change the atmosphere to be more like Earths so that plants could grow. Changing a planet like this is called **"terraforming"**

Small Objects
Comets, asteroids and meteoroids

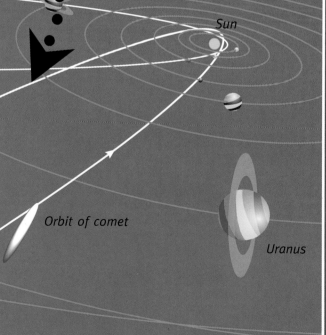

Asteroid 433 Eros, is 20 km long and 8 km wide. Eros is a near Earth asteroid (NEA)

What are comets?

Comets are huge balls of ice and dust, like a dirty snowball. They travel round the Sun and are usually named after the person of people who first discover them. Long ago people were afraid when they saw them, as they thought were a warning that something bad was going to happen.

Comet Hale-Bopp photographed from Merrit Island, Florida.

What are asteroids?

Asteroids are pieces of rock and metal that travel round the Sun and are too small to be considered planets. They are thought to be left over material from the formation of the solar system. There are millions of asteroids which range in size from a small pebble to giants like Ceres, which is around 1,000 km in diameter. A few asteroids even have their own Moons, such as the little asteroid Ida, which has its own Moon called Dactyl.

Why do comets have tails?

A comet far away from the Sun is just a solid block of dirty ice with no tail. As it gets closer to the Sun, it warms up and the outer layer melts. This forms a long trail of gas and dust behind the comet, forming a cloud called the coma. One of the most famous comets is **Halley's Comet** which is seen from Earth about once every 76 years. It was last seen in 1986, so will next be visible in 2062.

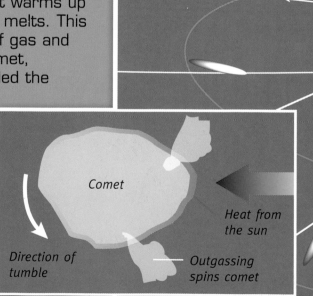

Comet

Direction of tumble

Heat from the sun

Outgassing spins comet

Sun

Orbit of comet

Uranus

What are "Shooting Stars"?

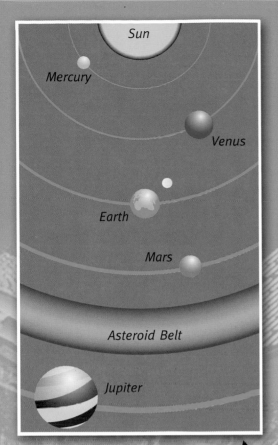

Meteoroids are small pieces of rock that are on a collision course with Earth. When a meteoroid hits the Earth's atmosphere at a high speed, **friction** makes it burn up in a streak of light called a meteor, or shooting star. Larger pieces of rock may not burn

The Leonid meteor shower arrives every year and can be spectacular. Photo courtesy of Bruce Johnson.

up completely and crash into the Earth. These are called meteorites. Meteorites range in size from tiny pebbles to huge boulders. A crater in Arizona, USA, is 1.2 km across and was probably made around 24 000 years ago by a meteorite.

What is the Asteroid Belt?

Nearly all asteroids are found in orbit between Jupiter and Mars. The gravity of these two planets keeps the asteroids locked into the Asteroid Belt. Illustrations of the Asteroid Belt often show thousands of asteroids close together, but in reality the space between asteroids is huge, making the belt mostly empty space.

Could an asteroid hit Earth?

It is not only possible, it has happened many times. The last big impact was at Tunguska in Russia in 1917. This was tiny compared to the asteroid that collided with Earth 65 million years ago and wiped out the dinosaurs. **Scientists** look out for large asteroids but they are difficult to spot, and at the moment we would not be able to stop one hitting the Earth.

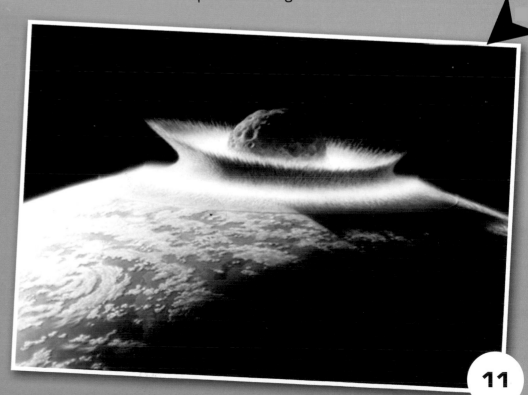

Fun Fact!

Comets do not give off their own light. What we see is Sunlight bouncing off the ice in the comet.

The Sun
and other stars

What are stars?

Stars are massive balls of burning **gas**. They are extremely hot and give off huge amounts of light and heat. Stars come in all different sizes, and although they all seem the same distance away from Earth, they are not. There are more stars in the Universe than anything else. There are so many that you could spend all your life counting them, and yet still would not have counted them all.

Each of these specks of light is a galaxy. Each galaxy contains roughly 100 billion stars. There are billions of galaxies in the visible universe.

Stars are different colours depending on how hot they are. Stars work in the same way as a fire does. The coolest part of a fire is the top where the flames are red. It is hotter in the middle where it glows yellow while the hottest part is near the fuel where it glows blue. Therefore some of the hottest stars are blue and are called Blue Giants. The biggest known stars are called Supergiants. Rigel is a blue supergiant which is over 100 times bigger than the Sun. Yellow stars like the Sun are a bit cooler, and are called Yellow Dwarfs. Red Dwarf stars are smaller and cooler than the Sun.

What is the Sun like?

The Sun is a medium-sized star but it could still fit more than a million Earths inside it. It is 1.4 million km in diameter and is the centre of the solar system, which the Earth and eight other planets go round. The Sun makes Sunlight by burning up four million tonnes of fuel every second. The temperature in the centre of the Sun is an unimaginable 15,000,000 degrees Celsius.

Fun Fact!

Stars can't be seen during the day because the Sun's light makes it too bright to see starlight, but they're still there.

What are supernovas?

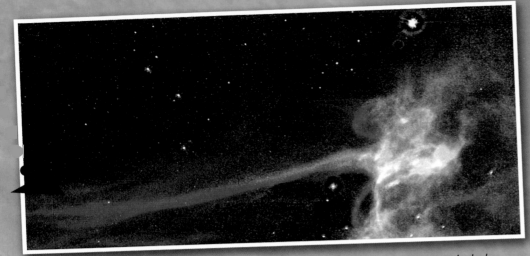

A ribbon of dust and gas is all that remains of an ancient supernova that exploded 15,000 years ago. The blast wave is moving outward at almost five million kilometres per hour. The supernova remnant is over 2,600 light years away, far outside our own galaxy.

Stars die when they run out of fuel to burn. Very large stars such as Blue Giants die in a huge explosion called a supernova. These can be seen as very bright stars in the night sky. Sometimes the explosion blows the star to bits, but sometimes the centre survives as a **neutron star** or black hole. Our Sun is too small to die as a supernova.

How do we study the Sun?

The Sun is so bright that it is very dangerous to look directly at it. It is even more dangerous to look at it through a telescope, you would be instantly blinded. Scientists study the Sun using a variety of safe viewing methods including projecting the Suns image onto a screen. Sun satellites study the Sun's magnetic field and often use **ultraviolet light** to take photographs as well. To protect the satellites delicate instruments a shield covers the bright disc of the Sun.

What causes a solar eclipse?

A solar eclipse happens when the Earth and Moon form a line with the Sun. When the Moon moves between the Earth and the Sun, part of the Sun's light is blocked by the Moon, and the sky slowly gets dark as the Moon moves in front of the Sun. A total eclipse occurs when the Moons **disc** completely covers the Sun. This can happen because although the Moon is 400 times smaller than the Sun it is also 400 times nearer the Earth. This strange coincidence means that both the Sun and the Moon appear the same size in the sky. During a total eclipse it becomes completely dark. A total eclipse is very rare and most people only see one in their lifetime.

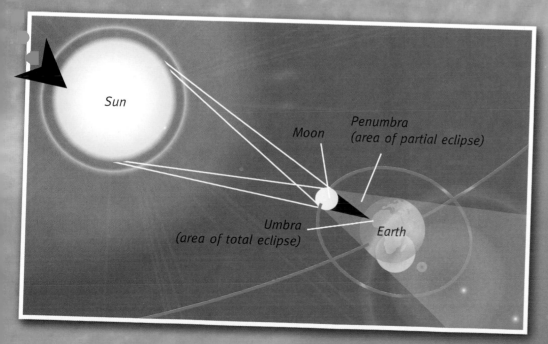

Sun

Moon

Penumbra
(area of partial eclipse)

Umbra
(area of total eclipse)

Earth

An image of solar flares from NASA's SOHO satellite. The circle in the centre of the image is the disc that protects the camera from the full brightness of the Sun and allows the fainter images to show up.

Mercury and Venus

What does the surface of Mercury look like?

Mercury looks similar to Earth's Moon. It is covered in craters, caused by rocks from space colliding into it millions of years ago. The biggest crater is called the Caloris Basin, which is more than 1,250 km across. The surface is baked hard by the extreme heat of the Sun. It is over 400 degrees Celsius in the daytime, but with little atmosphere to keep the heat in, nights are freezing cold, dropping to -200 degrees Celsius.

Fun Fact!

Because it is the innermost planet Mercury has the fastest orbit. It travels round the Sun at 167,400 km per hour.

How long is a year on Mercury?

How long a planet's day and years are depends on how close it is to the Sun, and how fast it spins around. A planet's year is the number of Earth days it takes to travel once around the Sun. A planet's day is how long it takes to spin around once. Because it is the closest planet to the Sun, a year on Mercury is only 88 days, but it spins round very slowly – each day on Mercury is 59 Earth days!

Which is the closest planet to the Sun?

If you travelled from Earth towards the Sun, the first planet you would meet would be Venus, which orbits at just over 108 million km from the Sun. Next you would arrive at Mercury, which at 58 million km is the closest planet to the Sun. Mercury is very small, the second smallest planet in the solar system.

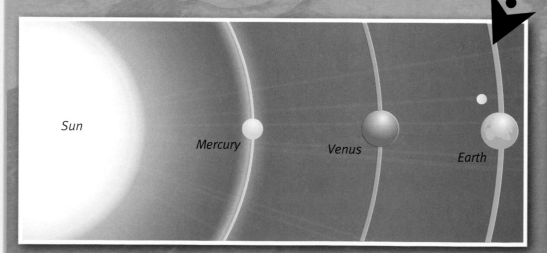

Sun

Mercury

Venus

Earth

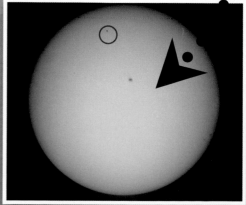

This tiny dot is the planet Mercury passing in front of the Sun. This is called a transit. It last happened in May 2003

What are the clouds on Venus made of?

Venus is covered in clouds so thick that its surface cannot be seen from Earth by even the most powerful telescopes. The clouds are made up mainly of **sulphuric acid** and are so dense that the atmospheric pressure is ninety times heavier than on Earth. This is about as heavy as being a kilometre under the sea on Earth. There are still active volcanoes on Venus and their eruptions send more poisonous chemicals into the atmosphere.

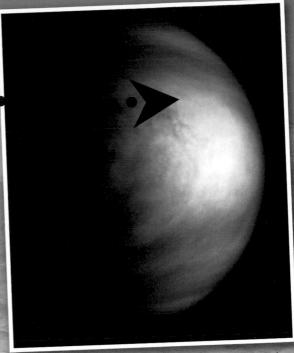

The clouds of Venus as seen from 2.7 million km away by the NASA probe Galileo

Why does Venus spin in the opposite direction to all the other planets?

On Venus, the Sun rises in the west and sets in the east, whereas on Earth the Sun rises in the east and sets in the west. This is because Venus spins in the opposite way to all the other planets. Nobody is quite sure why this happens, but scientists think that Venus may have been hit by another planet when it was forming, sending it spinning in the opposite direction. Venus is the slowest-spinning planet in the solar system. A day on Venus is 243 Earth days, and a year is only 225 Earth days, so a day is longer than a year on Venus!.

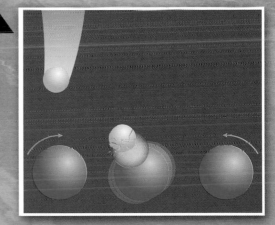

Which is the hottest planet?

Although it is further from the Sun than Mercury, the clouds on Venus trap the Sun's heat and prevent it escaping back into the atmosphere, making it the hottest planet. The temperature on Venus is about 465 degrees Celsius, hot enough to melt **lead**.

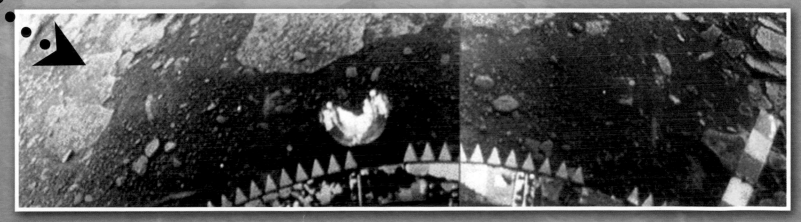

On the 1st of March 1982, NASA's Venera spacecraft landed on the planet Venus. The probe survived for just over two hours and sent back fourteen colour images of the surface before the intense heat melted it. The metal triangles at the bottom of the image is the spacecraft itself.

Jupiter and Saturn

Which is the biggest planet in the solar system?

By far the biggest planet in the solar system is Jupiter. If Jupiter was hollow all the other planets in the solar system could fit inside it. Not only is Jupiter the biggest planet, it also weighs more than twice as much as the rest of the planets in the solar system put together.

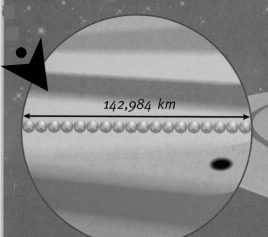

142,984 km

The diameter of Jupiter is 142,984km. The Earth has a diameter of 7,926 km. This means that Jupiter is slightly more than eighteen times wider than the Earth. However if Jupiter was hollow you could fit 1,400 Earths inside it.

How many Moons does Jupiter have?

Jupiter has around 61 Moons, but more are constantly being discovered. Some are only tiny "Moonlets" only a few kilometres in diameter. Ganymede is not only Jupiter's largest Moon, but the largest Moon in the solar system. Another large Moon is Io, which has constant volcanic eruptions, making it a very colourful Moon.

List of Jupiter's Moons as of February 2004

1. Metis	11. Himalia	29. Callirrhoe	47. S/2003 J7
2. Adrastea	12. Lysithea	30. Euporie	48. S/2003 J8
3. Amalthea	13. Elara	31. Kale	49. S/2003 J9
4. Thebe	14. S/2000 J11	32. Orthosie	50. S/2003 J10
5. Io	15. Iocaste	33. Thyone	51. S/2003 J11
6. Europa	16. Praxidike	34. Euanthe	52. S/2003 J12
7. Ganymede	17. Harpalyke	35. Hermippe	53. S/2003 J13
8. Callisto	18. Ananke	36. Pasithee	54. S/2003 J14
9. Themisto	19. Isonoe	37. Eurydome	55. S/2003 J15
10. Leda	20. Erinome	38. Aitne	56. S/2003 J16
	21. Taygete	39. Sponde	57. S/2003 J17
	22. Chaldene	40. Autonoe	58. S/2003 J18
	23. Carme	41. S/2003 J1	59. S/2003 J19
	24. Pasiphae	42. S/2003 J2	60. S/2003 J20
	25. S/2002 J1	43. S/2003 J3	61. S/2003 J21
	26. Kalyke	44. S/2003 J4	62. S/2003 J22
	27. Magaclite	45. S/2003 J5	
	28. Sinope	46. S/2003 J6	

What are Saturn's rings made of?

The rings around Saturn, which are easily seen even with a small telescope, are made of billions of chunks of ice and rocks. Some are as small as a speck of dust, others as large as a house. Scientists think these are the remains of a shattered Moon or comet. Although the rings are greater than 250,000 km across, they are less than a kilometre thick.

Why would Saturn float?

Although Saturn is the second largest planet in the solar system it is made up mostly of the gasses **hydrogen** and **helium** which are very light. This makes the whole planet less dense than water. If you had a bath big enough, then Saturn would float! All the other planets are denser than water and would sink.

Which is the only moon in the solar system with clouds?

Titan, the largest of Saturn's Moons, and one of the largest Moons in the solar system, is the only Moon with an atmosphere and clouds. Thick, dense clouds cover the whole of Titan. In fact its atmosphere is denser than Earth's, but it is made up of unbreathable **poisonous** gasses.

What is the Great Red Spot?

The Great Red Spot is a massive storm over twice the size of the Earth. It has been raging high in Jupiter's atmosphere for thousands of years. Scientists do not know how it's managed to last so long or if it will suddenly disappear.

Mysterious Titan, shrouded in orange clouds of methane gas.

The Outer Planets
Neptune, Uranus and Pluto

Why is Uranus a blue-green colour?

Like Jupiter and Saturn, Uranus is made entirely of gas and **liquid**. The outer layers are made of hydrogen, helium and methane. It is methane that gives Uranus its blue-green colour. Uranus is in the furthest parts of the solar system, and looks like a faint blue-green disc when seen through a telescope.

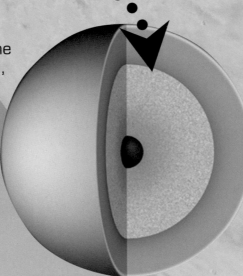

What is unusual about Neptune's Moon, Triton?

Triton is Neptune's largest Moon and is the only Moon in the solar system that moves in the opposite direction to the direction in which its planet spins. It's surface is made of dry ice and is the coldest surface known in the solar system, at -235 degrees **Celsius**.

Why does Uranus spin on its side?

Uranus is unique in the solar system, because unlike all the other planets and Moons, it spins on its side. Scientists think that millions of years ago Uranus may have been hit by a comet, tipping it on its side. Because of this tilt, Uranus has very unusual seasons.

Uranus and its ring photographed by the Hubble Space Telescope. Bands in the clouds are clearly visible.

Fun Fact!
A year on Neptune is 164.8 Earth years. So if you lived there it would take you nearly 1,500 years to reach your ninth birthday!

Which planet is furthest from the Sun?

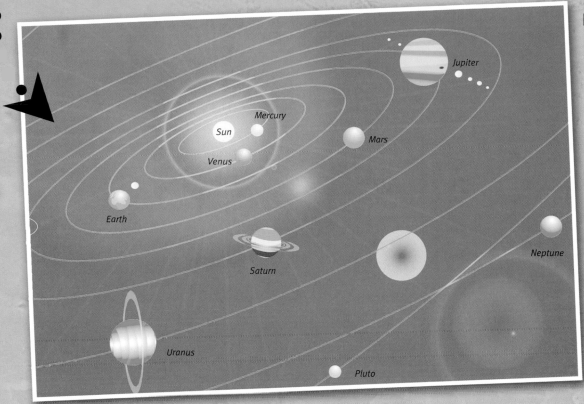

Diagram of the solar system showing the order of the planets. The planet's sizes and their orbits are not to scale.

Pluto is the outermost planet in the solar system, as it is 5.9 billion km from the Sun for most of its orbit. Measuring 320 km in diameter, it is also the smallest planet and has only one per cent of the volume of Earth. Because Pluto is so small, some scientists think it may not be a planet at all but a comet. Pluto's orbit is highly **elliptical** and for some of the time it crosses the orbit of Neptune making that planet the outermost member of the solar system.

What is beyond Pluto?

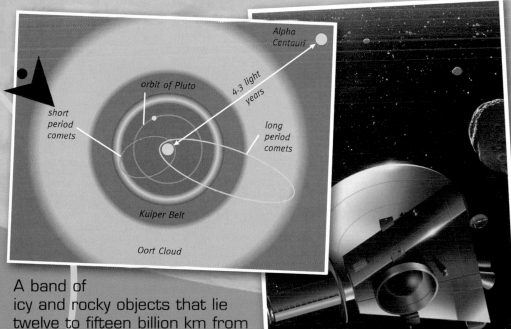

A band of icy and rocky objects that lie twelve to fifteen billion km from the Sun (twice as far as Pluto) make up the Kuiper Belt. Quaoar is one of the largest known objects in the Kuiper Belt and is only 1,290 km across. **NASA** is building a space probe called New Horizons to visit and explore this vast region of space. Out past the Kuiper Belt is the vast Oort Cloud, which is the home of countless billions of comets. The Oort Cloud extends for nearly three light years, or two thirds of the way to the nearest star.

Is there a ••• tenth planet? ••

There are millions of objects orbiting beyond Pluto in the Kuiper Belt. Scientists think they have discovered a new planet. They named it Sedna, after the Eskimo goddess of the sea.

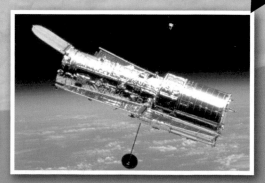

NASA use the Hubble Space telescope to look for planets around other stars.

Spacecraft

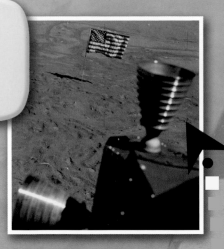

How do spacecraft get off the ground?

Anything that moves upwards from the Earth is pulled back by Earth's gravity. This is just like when you throw a ball in the air it will fall back to the ground. To escape the force of Earth's gravity, a spacecraft must travel extremely fast; 40,000 km per hour, or about fifty times faster than a jet airliner. The only engines that can do this are rockets.
Rockets need to carry oxygen because there is no oxygen in space and fuel needs oxygen to burn.

STS-75, the Shuttle Columbia, launches from Cape Canaveral. The shuttles three main engines develop over 0,6 million kg of thrust. An additional 1,3 million kg of thrust is produced by the two solid rocket boosters.

How do spacecraft steer in space?

Spacecraft use most of their energy or fuel getting off the ground. Once in space, there is no air so the spacecraft drifts along, using short bursts from smaller rockets placed around the spaceship to steer it around.

The shuttle Discovery landing at Edwards Air Force base.

What was the first reusable spacecraft?

The first rockets to travel to space could only be used once. This was extremely expensive, so space engineers built the reusable space shuttle. The space shuttle uses rockets to carry it into space. These rockets fall back to Earth and are re-used. The shuttle **glides** back through the Earth's atmosphere and lands on wheels like a plane.

Do all spacecraft carry people?

No, not all spacecraft carry people. Satellites and space probes are spacecraft that travel with no people in them. Some satellites are used to study space while others are used to carry phone messages and television pictures around the world. Space probes are **robots** controlled by computers on Earth. They have visited every planet in the solar system except Pluto.

Voyager 1 was launched in 1977 to visit both Jupiter and Saturn. It carries a plaque showing where it came from, and a recording of sounds from Earth, just in case it should be found by aliens

Fun Fact!

Voyager 1 is the furthest-travelled spacecraft and the most remote human object ever. It is currently over eight billion km away from Earth and on the verge of leaving the solar system.

What will future spacecraft be like? • • • • •

A new spacecraft called the X-33 is being developed to replace the space shuttle. The X-33 is an aeroplane that will fly to the top of the Earth's atmosphere, and then be propelled into outer space by a small rocket. This will be much cheaper than the space shuttle as it won't need a lot of expensive fuel to get into space. Cheaper flights into space could mean more people can visit space as **tourists**.

How long would it take to travel to the stars? • • • •

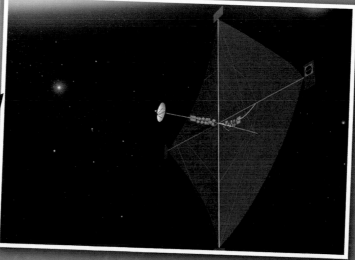

By accelerating slowly for a long period of time a solar-sail-powered spacecraft could reach half the speed of light, or more. Astronauts could reach the stars but the journeys would still take years.

The nearest star to Earth is a very long way away, over 39,900,000,000,000 km away. This would take our fastest rocket thousands of years to reach it.
Maybe future technology will design rockets capable of travelling much faster, enabling them to reach the stars in a shorter time.

···➤ The search for life

What is life?···

Life is all around us, but defining exactly what is alive and what is not is more difficult than you might think. Some non-living things can act like they are alive, while some living creatures can appear dead for thousands of years at a time. No-one knows if viruses are alive or not. All life on Earth is based on the molecule **DNA**. Viruses do not have DNA, they use the DNA of the host they infect.

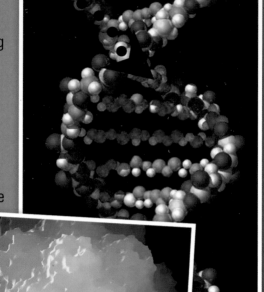

Ancient bacteria can remain in hibernation for millions of years before coming back to life. Viruses are very primitive life. They use the DNA of their hosts to reproduce, and can make humans, plants and animals ill in the process.

Are we alone?

As far as we know life only exists on our planet. Most scientists think that life must be common in the universe, but no sign of it has been found in our solar system or beyond. If we are alone, it means that life is an extraordinary thing and we must be extra careful to protect it.

The Earth as seen from space.

What is SETI?····

SETI stands for Search for Extraterrestrial Intelligence. The project was started in 1959 to search for radio signals from intelligent life in space. SETI uses **radio telescopes** around the world to look for patterns of radio waves in the sky. They also use computers connected to the internet in the search for alien life.

Where do scientists look for life?••••••

For many years scientists thought that life would exist on Earth-like planets. Now they believe life may be able to start in many sorts of places, as long as there is water. The most promising place in the solar system at the moment is Europa. This Moon of Jupiter may have a huge ocean of water under its icy surface. **Evidence** of past life may have been left on Mars, which also used to have water.

Under Europa's frozen surface scientists think there may be a huge ocean of liquid water (shown in blue). This water is kept liquid by heat generated by gravitation stress, due to Europa's close orbit to Jupiter. Unlike the Earth, Europa probably has a frozen metal core (shown in grey).

Does Mars have canals?••••••••••••

In the late 1800's two Italians observed straight lines on Mars which they called "canali". This was translated into English as "canal" instead of "channel". People began to think that canals had been made by intelligent life on Mars. It is now known that there are channels on Mars which look like Earth's river channels. Most scientists believe that water once flowed on Mars, but the channels are natural occurrences, not alien made.

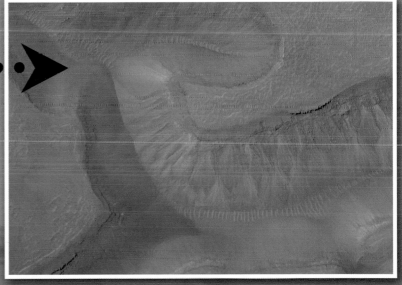

Water erosion features on Mars as pictured by NASA's Mars Global Surveyor orbiter ©NASA/JPL/Malin Space Science Systems.

•Will aliens look like us?

Humans are the product of **evolution** on our own specific planet, so the chances of aliens looking anything like us is virtually nil. How aliens look will depend on the conditions on their home. If they exist they will look far stranger than they appear on TV or films. In fact they will probably be stranger than we can even imagine!

Deep Space

What is the Milky Way?

The Milky Way is the spiral-shaped galaxy that we live in. There are 200 billion stars, including the Sun, in the Milky Way and Earth is positioned out on one of the spiral arms. Our galaxy is 100,000 light years across. If you look into the sky where there is no **light pollution**, (man-made light drowning out the light of the stars) you can sometimes see a faint glowing band which is the bright centre of the Milky Way.

The Milky Way as seen from Earth on a clear night.

What are galaxies?

Galaxies are huge collections of stars held together by gravity. They can contain anything from a few million to 400 **billion** stars, and come in a variety of types including lens-shaped, spiral and elliptical galaxies. Galaxies are grouped together in clusters. Our Milky Way is part of what is called the Local Cluster. The nearest Galaxy to ours is called Andromeda. It is between 2-3 million light years away and is the furthest object visible to the human eye.

What is a light year?

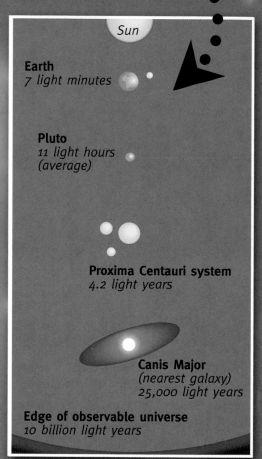

Sun

Earth
7 light minutes

Pluto
11 light hours (average)

Proxima Centauri system
4.2 light years

Canis Major
(nearest galaxy)
25,000 light years

Edge of observable universe
10 billion light years

A light year is what astronomers use to measure distances in space. Light is faster than anything else. It travels at a speed of 300,000 km a second, or seven times round the Earth in one second. A light year is the distance that light can travel in one year. This is around 9,460 million km.

The Hubble Space Telescope takes a picture of a nearby elliptical galaxy (like the Milky Way) from sideways on.

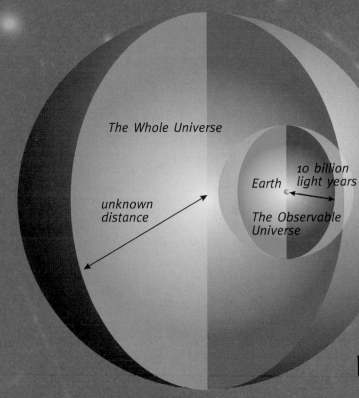

The Whole Universe

Earth

10 billion light years

unknown distance

The Observable Universe

How big is the universe?

The Observable Universe is a **sphere** ten billion light years across, centred on the Earth. The Whole Universe is many times bigger than this, but there has not been enough time since the Big Bang for the light to reach us so it will remain forever invisible.

Are there planets round other stars?

What is the furthest visible object?

At the furthest edge of the Observable Universe are very bright, powerful objects called **quasars**. These are probably giant black holes that swallow stars. Because they are so far from Earth, it takes billions of years for their light to reach us. Beyond them is the background microwave radiation, which is the left-over heat from the Big Bang when the universe was only 300,000 years old.

Many of the stars you can see have planets orbiting them. Because the stars are so far away, it is impossible to see the planets, so scientists have worked out several clever ways to find them. In one method scientists look to see if the star is wobbling. This wobble is caused by the gravity of any planet that might be in orbit. Another method is to watch to see if a star suddenly dims then brightens again. This may be caused by a planet moving in front of the star and blocking some of the light. By 2004 scientists had discovered 104 planetary systems with a total of 119 planets. More are discovered every year.

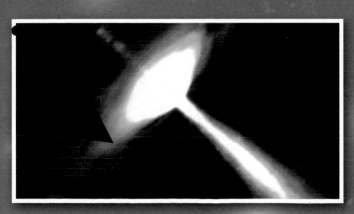

Quasars emit powerful bursts of radiation making them amongst the brightest objects in the universe. This means that they can still be seen, even though they are so small and far away

Fun Fact!

The furthest planet ever found in the Milky Way, OGLE-TR-56B, was discovered in 2003. Travelling at the speed of light it would take 5,000 years to reach.

Studying space

What is the world's largest telescope?

The largest telescope in the world is the Arecibo radio telescope in Puerto Rico. Its dish is 305m wide and is used by astronomers for studying the Universe. It can also send radio waves and broadcast messages that might be heard by **extraterrestrial** life.

The Arecibo dish is built into a mountainside in Puerto Rico. The dish is operated by Cornell University in the USA.

Why are telescopes often built on mountain tops?

Not to be nearer space, but to be above as much atmosphere as possible. The atmosphere is what makes the stars twinkle and it spoils the pictures that astronomers want to take. The air on the top of mountains, particularly near the **equator**, is clearer and stiller so the telescopes can see more clearly.

The telescope at Cerro Pachon, Chile.

What are satellites?

Satellites are objects that orbit or go around another object. Man-made satellites are space ships that are controlled from Earth and are used to explore the Universe. They are used for weather forecasting, sending television pictures, phone messages, e-mails and web pages around the world.

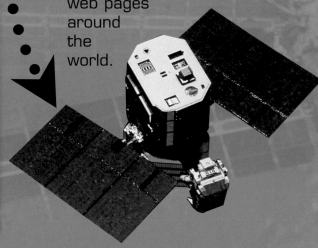

What is radio astronomy?•••••••••••➤

Normal or optical telescopes use light to look at the stars. For some objects this is not the best way to see them. Scientists use radio telescopes to view distant galaxies, because it is easier to build large collecting dishes than large mirrors. Radio telescopes can be very large, most have steerable dishes to allow astronomers to look at different parts of the sky.

Jodrell bank in England is one of the largest steerable radio dishes in the world. The telescope is over 40 years old.

Which telescope wears glasses?•

the Hubble Space Telescope

When it was first launched, the mirror in the Hubble Space Telescope had a flaw in it that meant that the telescope was slightly out of **focus**. NASA sent a shuttle up and astronauts fitted a correcting mirror to the telescope, just like an optician fitting glasses. Now Hubble focuses perfectly, and provides the clearest views of deep space objects.

Fun Fact!
Future telescope: the VLT (very large telescope), will consist of four telescopes measuring eight metres each. This is the equivalent of one thirty-two metre telescope!

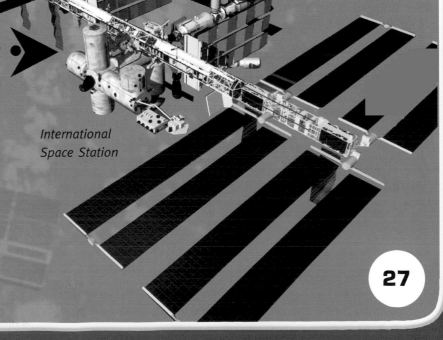

International Space Station

Where are experiments performed in space?

In order to perform experiments scientists need a laboratory. The first space laboratories were the American Skylab and the Russian **space station** Mir. Both have since re-entered the atmosphere and been destroyed. The international space station is still being built by eleven nations, but several astronauts already call it home. It will take many more years to finish.

Space People

Who were the crew of the first Moon landing?

Buzz Aldrin
Neil Armstrong
Michael Collins

There were three crew members on the historical first flight to the Moon in July 1969. One of the crew, Michael Collins, stayed with the **command module**, "Columbia", while the other two men landed on the Moon in the lunar module, "Eagle". The first man to step onto the Moon was Neil Armstrong, who was followed by Buzz Aldrin. The two men spent 21 hours on the Moon, collecting rocks and performing experiments.

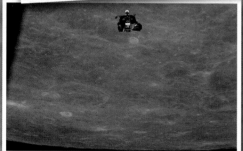
Lunar module landing on the Moon

Buzz Aldrin walking on the Moon

Neil Armstrong pictured in Buzz Aldrin's faceplate

Who invented the telescope?

A spectacle-maker in Holland, Hans Lippershey, invented the telescope in 1608. He got the idea from two children who were playing with lenses in his shop. They noticed that the weather vane on the church nearby became larger when they held two lenses together. Lippershey tried it with a tube between the lenses and the telescope was invented.

Who discovered the last planet, Pluto?

Pluto was discovered in 1930 by an American astronomer called Clyde William Tombaugh, who was looking for the mystery ninth planet, but in the wrong place. Pluto is so distant that even the Hubble telescope can only **resolve** a small blurred image of it. Pluto is the only planet in the solar system never to have been visited by a space probe. This will change in 2016 when NASA hopes to land a small probe on the surface.

Who was the first man in space? ....

The first man in space was a Russian named Yuri Gagarin. On April 12th, 1961, he flew once round the Earth at a speed of 27,400 km per hour in the spaceship Vostok 1. After 108 minutes he **ejected** from the spaceship and landed by parachute to become a national and international hero. He was killed in a plane crash in 1968.

Fun Fact!

A special pen with rubber-like ink was invented for astronauts so that they could write in space. The pen also works underwater.

Who was the last man on the Moon?

The last person to stand on the Moon was Eugene Cernan, who flew to the Moon in Apollo 17 in December 1972. Since then nobody has been further into space than low Earth orbit. In 2004, US president George W. Bush announced that America would return to the Moon and go on to Mars. So, hopefully, one day, man will return to the Moon.

Who was Laika?

Laika was the first living creature to go into space. She was a three-year old mongrel dog whose name meant "Barker" in Russian. Laika's original name was Kudryavka (Little Curly), but this was changed by the Russian space programme. On November 3rd, 1957 she was sent into space on the Sputnik 2 by the **Soviet Union**. There was no way of returning Laika to Earth and so she died in space a few days later.

Laika in her pressurised cabin just before lift off.

Glossary

© 2006 Creations for Children International, Belgium. www.c4ci.com
Written by Diane Stephens.
Designed by Meme Ltd, UK.
All rights reserved.
Printed in China.

Astronaut
The American word for a person who is trained to fly into space. Russian astronauts are known as Cosmonauts.

Big Bang
The name for the popular theory of the creation of the universe. All the matter in the universe started out squeezed in one tiny space smaller than an atom. The universe was created when this exploded outwards creating the universe as we know it today.

Billion
In America a billion is a thousand million. In Europe a billion is a million million. This book uses American billions.

Carbon dioxide
A poisonous gas that is responsible for the greenhouse effect on Venus and Earth too. It is made by combining one carbon and two oxygen atoms. Carbon dioxide makes up 0.003 percent of the Earth's atmosphere.

Celsius
A measurement of temperature, invented by Anders Celsius in 1742. America uses the Fahrenheit scale. 0 degrees Celsius is the freezing point of water. 100 degrees Celsius is the boiling point of water.

Command module
The part of the Apollo Moon mission that remained in orbit around the Moon as a link between the Moon's surface and mission control on Earth. The lander (LEM) was attached to the front of the command module.

Coral reef
A giant organism consisting of billions of individual polyps whose hard outer skeleton make up the bulk of the reef. Coral reefs are a delicate organism that are under threat from pollution and global warming.

Core
The centre of a planet is known as the core. The rocky inner planets have molten, iron-rich cores while the outer gas giants have frozen metallic cores.

Disc
The circular outline of a Moon or planet is called a disc. Planetary discs need a telescope to be visible.

DNA
Deoxyribonucleic acid. DNA is the famous double helix molecule that contains all the genetic information needed to recreate a new organism.

Ejected
Pilots are ejected from their planes if they are going to crash. They use a special ejection seat which uses rockets to boost the pilot clear of the craft.

Elliptical
A type of orbit that is not completely circular but slightly flattened. Planets move in slightly elliptical orbits. Pluto's orbit is highly elliptical, as are comets, which is why some people think Pluto may actually be a large comet.

Equator
The imaginary great circle around the Earth's surface, equidistant from the poles and perpendicular to the Earth's axis of rotation. It divides the Earth into the Northern Hemisphere and the Southern Hemisphere.

Evidence
Scientists look for evidence to prove their theories. Without evidence they cannot prove whether their ideas are correct or merely guesswork.

Evolution
The process by which species adapt to new environments. Random genetic mutations result in offspring that are more suited to conditions than their siblings. These traits are then passed on to subsequent generations.

Experiments
Scientist devise and carry out experiments in order to give them the evidence they need to prove their theories. Experiments must be easily repeatable by other scientists in order to check the results.

Extraterrestrial
Not from our world. Often used to describe alien life forms. but it refers to anything from an other planet such as rocks or atmosphere.

Focus
Telescopes need to focus, just like cameras. When the telescope is focused the image is sharp and detailed. The Hubble Space Telescope uses an extra corrective mirror to allow it to focus properly.

Friction
The force that causes objects to heat up on entering the Earth's atmosphere. Friction is caused by the resistance of the air in the atmosphere. Smooth objects generate less friction which is why ice is slippery.

Gas
One of the states of matter. In gas the atoms are loosely packed allowing them to move freely.

Glide
Planes without engines glide. A glider's wings are designed to be very efficient to make best use of the lift generated. The Space Shuttle is a very poor glider but it flies so fast that it can stay in the air long enough to land safely.

Halley's Comet
The most famous comet. Halley's Comet was known by the ancient Chinese and appears in the Bayeux Tapestry. It is a short period comet that returns every 76 years.